GREAT IMPRESSIONIST PAINTINGS

POSTCARD BOOK

THE NATIONAL GALLERY, LONDON

Front cover illustration
A detail from **A Wheatfield, with Cypresses**
Vincent van Gogh 1853–1890
Canvas, 72.1 x 90.9 cm

© National Gallery Publications Limited 1995
5/6 Pall Mall East, London SW1Y 5BA

Reprinted 1995, 1996

Printed in Singapore by Imago Publishing Limited

NGPL Stock Number 301029

ISBN 1 85709 077 2

The National Gallery houses one of the world's finest collections of Western European painting from about 1260 to 1920. It was founded in 1824 when Parliament voted £57,000 for the purchase of 38 pictures from the collection of John Julius Angerstein, a financier and Russian emigré. Among the paintings were five Claudes, two Rembrandts, Raphael's *Julius II*, Hogarth's *Marriage à La Mode* series, and Sebastiano del Piombo's *Raising of Lazarus* (still inventoried as No. 1). Other purchases and bequests quickly followed.

At first the national collection hung in Angerstein's house at 100 Pall Mall. It moved to the present building, designed by William Wilkins, in 1838. Since then the building has been greatly extended to accommodate the growing collection. The most significant recent addition is the Sainsbury Wing, designed by Robert Venturi of Venturi, Scott Brown Associates Inc, of Philadelphia, USA, which was opened by HM The Queen in 1991. This wing provides new galleries for the Early Renaissance collection as well as temporary exhibition galleries, a lecture theatre, a computer information room, and a restaurant and shop.

Today the collection contains over 2,250 paintings and is visited by some four million people every year.

Visitors' Information

The National Gallery
Trafalgar Square, London WC2N 5DN
Telephone 0171-839 3321
Information 0171-747 2885
Admission free

Open

Monday to Saturday: 10am to 6pm
Sunday: 2pm to 6pm
Closed: New Year's Day, Good Friday, Christmas
Eve, Christmas Day and Boxing Day.

Shops

Monday to Saturday: 10am to 5.40pm
Sunday: 2pm to 5.40pm (last admission 5.30pm)

Micro Gallery

Computer Information Room (sponsored by
American Express Foundation)
Monday to Saturday: 10am to 5.30pm
Sunday: 2pm to 5.30pm

Brasserie and Café

The Brasserie in the Sainsbury Wing and the Café
in the main building are open Monday to Saturday:
10am to 5pm, Sunday: 2pm to 5pm

Disabled visitors

Access at the Sainsbury Wing or Orange Street
entrances where lifts to all floors are situated.
Wheelchairs are available on request. The
Sainsbury Wing Theatre is equipped with an
induction loop system to assist the hard of
hearing.

Lectures, films and free guided tours

For details of these and other Gallery events see the
current *National Gallery News* or ask at the
Information Desks.

Hillside in Provence

Paul Cézanne 1839-1906

Canvas, 63.5 x 79.4 cm

THE NATIONAL GALLERY
© National Gallery Publications Limited

Ballet Dancers

Edgar Degas 1834-1917

Canvas, 72.4 x 73 cm

THE NATIONAL GALLERY
© National Gallery Publications Limited

The Museum at Le Havre

Claude Monet 1840-1926
Canvas, 75 x 100 cm

THE NATIONAL GALLERY
© National Gallery Publications Limited

Bathers at Asnières

Georges Seurat 1859-1891
Canvas, 201 x 300 cm

THE NATIONAL GALLERY
© National Gallery Publications Limited

Self Portrait

Paul Cézanne 1839-1906

Canvas, 33.6 x 26 cm

THE NATIONAL GALLERY
© National Gallery Publications Limited

Flood Waters

Claude Monet 1840-1926

Canvas, 71 x 91.5 cm

THE NATIONAL GALLERY
© National Gallery Publications Limited

A Wheatfield, with Cypresses

Vincent van Gogh 1853-1890
Canvas, 72.1 x 90.9 cm

THE NATIONAL GALLERY
© National Gallery Publications Limited

View from Louveciennes

Camille Pissarro 1830-1903

Canvas, 52.7 x 81.9 cm

THE NATIONAL GALLERY

Tiger in a Tropical Storm (Surprised!)

Henri Rousseau 1844-1910

Canvas, 129.8 x 161.9 cm

THE NATIONAL GALLERY
© National Gallery Publications Limited

The Gare St-Lazare

Claude Monet 1840-1926
Canvas, 54.3 x 73.6 cm

THE NATIONAL GALLERY

A Vase of Flowers

Paul Gauguin 1848-1903

Canvas, 64 x 74 cm

THE NATIONAL GALLERY
© National Gallery Publications Limited

Long Grass with Butterflies

Vincent van Gogh 1853-1890

Canvas, 64.5 x 80.7 cm

THE NATIONAL GALLERY
© National Gallery Publications Limited

The Petit Bras of the Seine at Argenteuil

Claude Monet 1840-1926

Canvas, 52.6 x 71.8 cm

Ophelia among the Flowers

Odilon Redon 1840-1916

Pastel on paper, 64 x 91 cm

THE NATIONAL GALLERY
© National Gallery Publications Limited

The Côte des Bœufs at L'Hermitage

Camille Pissarro 1830-1903

Canvas, 114.9 x 87.6 cm

THE NATIONAL GALLERY
© National Gallery Publications Limited

Sunflowers

Vincent van Gogh 1853-1890

Canvas, 92.1 x 73 cm

THE NATIONAL GALLERY
© National Gallery Publications Limited

Bathers at La Grenouillère

Claude Monet 1840-1926
Canvas, 73 x 92 cm

THE NATIONAL GALLERY
© National Gallery Publications Limited

After the Bath, Woman drying herself

Edgar Degas 1834-1917
Pastel on paper, 103.8 x 98.4 cm

THE NATIONAL GALLERY
© National Gallery Publications Limited

The Umbrellas

Pierre-Auguste Renoir 1841-1919
Canvas, 180.3 x 114.9 cm

THE NATIONAL GALLERY
© National Gallery Publications Limited

Bathers (Les Grandes Baigneuses)

Paul Cézanne 1839-1906

Canvas, 127.2 x 196.1 cm

THE NATIONAL GALLERY

Summer's Day

Berthe Morisot 1841–1895

Canvas, 45.7 x 75.2 cm

THE NATIONAL GALLERY
© National Gallery Publications Limited

Boating on the Seine

Pierre-Auguste Renoir 1841-1919

Canvas, 71 x 92 cm

THE NATIONAL GALLERY

Music in the Tuileries Gardens

Edouard Manet 1832-1883

Canvas, 76.2 x 118.1 cm

THE NATIONAL GALLERY

The Boulevard Montmartre at Night

Camille Pissarro 1830-1903

Canvas, 53.3 x 64.8 cm

Van Gogh's Chair

Vincent van Gogh 1853-1890

Canvas, 91.8 x 73 cm

THE NATIONAL GALLERY

The Beach at Trouville

Claude Monet 1840–1926

Canvas, 37.5 x 45.7 cm

THE NATIONAL GALLERY
© National Gallery Publications Limited